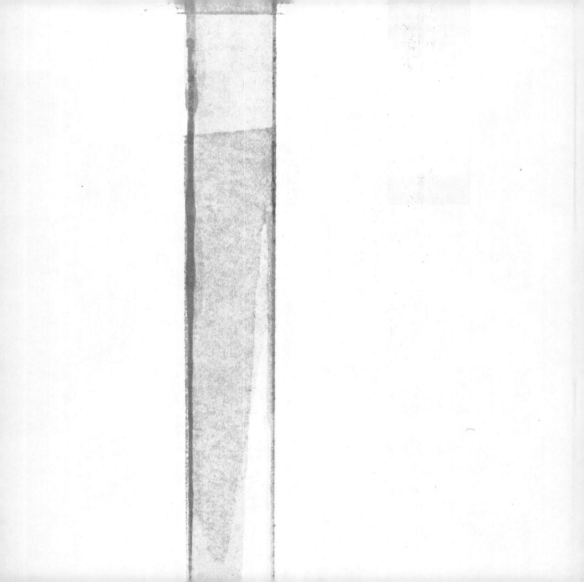

BERRIES

BERRIES

A BOOK OF RECIPES

EDITED BY: HELEN SUDELL

LORENZ BOOKS

First published in 2014 by Lorenz Books
an imprint of Anness Publishing Limited
108 Great Russell Street, London WC1B 3NA
www.annesspublishing.com
www.lorenzbooks.com; info@anness.com

If you like the images in this book and would like to investigate
using them for publishing, promotions or advertising, please visit
our website www.practicalpictures.com for more information

A CIP catalogue record for this book is available from
The British Library

Publisher Joanna Lorenz
Editorial Director Helen Sudell
Designer Nigel Partridge
Illustrations Anna Koska

Printed and bound in China

COOK'S NOTES

· Bracketed terms are intended for American readers.

· For all recipes, quantities are given in both metric and imperial
measures and, where appropriate, in standard cups and spoons.
Follow one set of measures, but not a mixture, because they are
not interchangeable.

· Standard spoon and cup measures are level. 1 tsp = 5ml,
1 tbsp = 15ml, 1 cup = 250ml/8fl oz.

· Australian standard tablespoons are 20ml. Australian readers
should use 3 tsp in place of 1 tbsp for measuring small quantities.

· American pints are 16fl oz/2 cups. American readers should use
20fl oz/2.5 cups in place of 1 pint when measuring liquids.

· Electric oven temperatures in this book are for conventional
ovens. When using a fan oven, the temperature will probably need
to be reduced by about 10–20°C/20–40°F. Since ovens vary, you
should check with your manufacturer's instruction book for
guidance.

· The nutritional analysis given for each recipe is calculated per
portion (i.e. serving or item), unless otherwise stated. If the recipe
gives a range, such as Serves 4–6, then the nutritional analysis will
be for the smaller portion size, i.e. 6 servings. The analysis does not
include optional ingredients, such as salt added to taste.

· Medium (US large) eggs are used unless otherwise stated.

PUBLISHER'S NOTE

CONTENTS

INTRODUCTION

Berries are the very essence of summer. The first sight of those bright colours in the shops inevitably conjures up thoughts of long, summer days; of picnics in the country and on the beach; of leisurely lunches and garden parties – and we long to begin eating just-picked fruit from a basket or even straight off the stem.

First among the berries to arrive are strawberries. Even

Below: There is nothing to beat the taste of home-grown fruit.

though glass-grown strawberries are in the shops year-round, the first home-grown strawberries symbolize par excellence the arrival of summer sunshine. And strawberries are perfect for all summer occasions, whether it's a wedding breakfast, smart reception or just lunch for family and friends in the garden. Strawberries have a long history of delighting us: "Doubtless God could have invented a better berry" said a sixteenth-century aficionado, "but doubtless he never did". In 1812, Dolly Madison, wife of the fourth US president and famous hostess, served strawberries picked from her own garden at the President's second Inaugural Ball at the White House. The first strawberries were tiny wild ones, like today's *fraises des bois*; the luscious monsters we now eat have been developed over the centuries.

Above: Picking blackberries is one of the joys of autumn.

Strawberries and raspberries both have their admirers. Perfection depends a little on the temperature zone you live in, as well as personal preference: strawberries need maximum sun but raspberries prefer a winter frost and a wetter climate.

Berries are wild fruits and there is a rich harvest to be had, varying with the season: currants of all colours, blackberries, blueberries and bilberries, and even raspberries of different colours. If you don't have the room to grow your own soft fruit you can always pick baskets of them at your nearest fruit farm.

HEALTHY PROPERTIES

Berries are some of the most powerful disease-fighting foods available. As well as being packed full of vitamin C, scientists have found that berries have some of the highest antioxidant levels of any fresh fruits. Antioxidants

Below: Fresh berries make a delightful topping for cakes.

work hard to protect the body by neutralizing free radicals, which can damage the cells that are a major source of disease and aging. They are also rich in dietary fibre, which helps to maintain a healthy gastro-intestinal tract, lowers blood cholesterol, reduces heart disease and may prevent certain types of cancers.

SERVING IDEAS

Many berries, such as strawberries, raspberries and blueberries are naturally sweet and are best served with cream or crème fraîche and perhaps a little sugar. Their brilliant colours make them perfect decorative accompaniments to cakes and creamy desserts. Berries also make vibrant and flavourful purées and sauces which are delicious poured over ice cream or served with desserts and cakes.

Some berries are more tart in flavour and make natural partners with meat and fish. Cranberries, lingonberries and

Above: Juicy berries make cool, refreshing drinks.

redcurrants are excellent for creating a piquant sauce to accompany poultry or to balance rich meats.

Berries also make refreshing smoothies. Mix together fresh berries and low-fat yogurt or milk and you have an instantly satisfying start to the day.

Finally, berries are perfect for making jams and jellies to keep you going through the long winter months, still savouring the sweet summer tastes of fresh berries.

BERRY VARIETIES

Berries come in all shapes and colours and all have different flavours and uses in the kitchen.

BLACKBERRIES
Also called a bramble because it grows on bushes with thorns, the blackberry is a sweet, juicy black fruit made up of many tiny segments, each containing a tiny seed. Ripe blackberries can be eaten raw straight off the branch, but they are best after cooking, which softens the seeds and deepens the flavour. In the same family of plants, there is a trailing type known as dewberries. These berries have a similar flavour to blackberries and are very juicy.

STRAWBERRIES
A large, bright red fruit with an intense scented fragrance, the cultivated strawberry has been developed from crossbreeding a small wild American strawberry and a juicy variety from South America. Wild strawberries (*Fraises des bois*) are also widely cultivated and are prized for their aroma. Strawberries are delicious served with cream or macerated in champagne, red wine or orange juice. They can be puréed to make a cold sauce or soup and can be used in dishes which only require short cooking, such as crème brûlée. Nowadays, strawberries are available all year round.

BLUEBERRIES
This small, round, firm, purplish blue fruit is juicy and sweet, with a mild flavour, and is used in pies, jams and cheesecakes, or just eaten raw with sour cream. Bilberries, which grow wild in may parts of Europe, are members of the same family, but are much smaller and have a sharp, fragrant taste.

CRANBERRIES
This smooth, bright red berry is very hard and sour, but once sweetened can be used in both sweet and savoury dishes. It makes an excellent piquant sauce for meat and poultry. Cranberries belong to the same

plant family as the blueberry. Another relative, originally from Scandinavia, is the lingonberry. Smaller than the cranberry, it has the same tart flavour. Cranberries can be substituted with lingonberries in any recipe.

CURRANTS

Blackcurrants and redcurrants are both small, tart berries which make wonderful jams, jellies and sauces to serve with

meat and game dishes. The shiny, bright appearance of redcurrants also makes them an attractive addition to desserts. Blackcurrants are best cooked and when sweetened have an intense tangy flavour.

RASPBERRIES

These deep red fruits are prized for their delicate flavour. Their soft texture means that they don't need cooking and they are popular as a decoration and filling for meringues and gâteaux. They can, of course, be cooked and make a wonderful filling for hot pies, especially when combined with apples. Crushed and sieved (strained), they make a lovely fruity sauce to serve with ice cream.

A rarely cultivated type of raspberry is the Scandinavian cloudberry, a pink berry with a sweet taste. The salmonberry is a wild raspberry found in North America. The large berries are a salmon-pink colour and they can be stewed or used instead of raspberries. The thimbleberry is a thimble-shaped American raspberry which is light red in colour and has a good taste.

GOOSEBERRIES

The gooseberry, a cousin of the blackcurrant, is native to Europe and North America. The fruits come in many varieties, some hard and sour, others sweeter. They make a wonderful sauce to serve with rich, oily fish.

COOKING WITH BERRIES

Most berries need very little cleaning: just remove tops and stalks where appropriate and discard any soft, mouldy or very unripe berries.

Avoid washing them; a wipe with a piece of damp kitchen paper should suffice.

FREEZING BERRIES

Open-freeze perfect specimens in a single layer then pack into rigid containers.

PURÉEING BERRIES

Berries can be puréed for sauces, fools and sorbets.

Briefly wash the berries and push through a fine nylon sieve (strainer), using the back of a large spoon or ladle. For a coarser purée, mash cooked berries with a potato masher.

PREPARING A COULIS

A coulis is always made using uncooked fruit.

Rinse the berries and transfer to a bowl. Crush the berries to a purée with a fork. Tip into a sieve (strainer) set over a clean bowl. Rub through, using the back of a large spoon. Sweeten to taste with sugar and stir well.

REDCURRANT JELLY

This jewel-like jelly is the traditional accompaniment to lamb and venison.

Put the redcurrants (as many as you have) in a pan with just enough water to cover. Simmer for 8–10 minutes or until the currants are very soft.

Strain through a jelly bag, then measure the liquid. Pour it back into the pan and add 350g/12oz/ 1½ cups granulated (white) sugar for every 600ml/20fl oz/ 2½ cups liquid. Stir over heat until dissolved. Boil briskly until setting point is reached (see page 13), skimming off any scum as it rises. Pour into sterilized jars, seal and label.

CRANBERRY SAUCE

This famous sauce is served with turkey or rich, red meats.

Thinly pare an orange, taking care to remove only the zest. Squeeze the juice and put it in a pan with the zest.

Add 350g/12oz/3 cups berries and cook gently for a few minutes until the skins pop.

Stir in sugar to taste and simmer for 5 minutes. Pour the sauce into a bowl, allow to cool and then chill before serving.

CRANBERRY AND CHESTNUT STUFFING

This is the traditional Christmas stuffing for turkey.

Makes about 450g/1lb

Soften 115g/4oz finely chopped onion in 25g/1oz butter in a pan. Stir in 175g/6oz unsweetened chestnut purée and 30ml/2 tbsp cooked cranberries. Season to taste with salt and black pepper and mix thoroughly. Take off the heat and stir in 225g/8oz fresh white breadcrumbs. Chop 115g/4oz canned chestnuts and fold into the mixture. Leave to cool completely before stuffing the bird.

BLACKBERRY AND APPLE CHEESE

An intensely rich, dark preserve.

Makes about 900g/2lb

Put 900g/2lb/7 cups blackberries, 450g/1lb chopped cooking apples and juice and rind of 1 lemon in a pan. Half-cover with water, bring to the boil and simmer for 15 minutes. Cool then push through a sieve. Measure the purée into a pan adding 400g/14oz/2 cups warmed granulated (white) sugar for every 600ml/20fl oz/2½ cups purée. Heat the purée, stirring until the sugar dissolves. Cook for 40 minutes until very thick. Spoon into sterilized jars, seal and label.

PRESERVES AND SWEET TREATS

Seasonal berries make excellent preserves and will store well for 6 months in a cool, dark place.

RASPBERRY JAM
This is the queen of jams.

Makes about 3.6kg/8lb
Put 1.8kg/4lb/13 cups raspberries into a preserving pan with the juice of 1 lemon and simmer until soft. Add 1.8kg/4lb/8 cups warmed granulated (white) sugar and stir until dissolved, then bring back to the boil and boil until setting point is reached, testing after 3–4 minutes. Pour into warmed, sterilized jars.

GARDEN JAM
A delicious mix of summer fruits makes a perfect preserve.

Makes about 3.6kg/8lb
Put 450g/1lb/3 cups blackcurrants into a large preserving pan and add 150ml/5fl oz/²/₃ cup water. Bring to the boil and simmer until almost cooked. Add 450g/1lb/3 cups each of blackberries, raspberries and strawberries and simmer gently, stirring occasionally, for 10 minutes or until the fruit is just soft. Add 1.8kg/4lb/8 cups warmed granulated (white)

sugar to the pan and stir over a gentle heat until dissolved. Bring to the boil and boil hard until setting point is reached. Pour into sterilized, warm jars. Cover and seal.

WILD STRAWBERRY AND ROSE PETAL CONSERVE
This fragrant jam is ideal served with summer cream teas.

Makes 900g/2lb
Put 900g/2lb/7 cups wild strawberries in a non-metallic bowl with the petals from 2 dark pink rosebuds, the juice of 2 lemons and 1.3kg/3lb/6 cups warmed granulated (white)

sugar. Cover overnight. The next day, tip the fruit into a preserving pan and heat gently, stirring, until all the sugar has dissolved. Boil for 10–15 minutes, or until setting point has been reached. Stir in a few drops of rosewater, then remove from the heat. Skim off any scum, then stir and pour into warmed sterilized jars.

SETTING POINT

To test if jam or jelly has set, put a spoonful on to a cold saucer. Allow it to cool slightly, then push the surface of the jam with your finger. Setting point has been reached if a skin has formed and it wrinkles. If not, boil for a little longer and keep testing regularly until it sets.

BLACKBERRY AND SLOE JELLY

This preserve is delicious served with roast meats, such as lamb.

Makes 1.3kg/3lb

Wash 450g/1lb/3 cups sloes (black plums), prick them, put them in a large heavy pan with 600ml/20fl oz/2½ cups water and bring to the boil. Reduce the heat, cover and simmer for 5 minutes. Rinse 1.8kg/4lb/13 cups blackberries and add them to the pan with the juice of 1 lemon. Bring the mixture back to a simmer and cook gently for 20 minutes, or until the fruit is very soft.

Pour the fruit and juices into a sterilized jelly bag suspended over a large non-metallic bowl. Leave to drain several hours, until the juices have stopped dripping. Measure the fruit juice into a preserving pan, adding 450g/1lb/2½ cups granulated (white) sugar for every 600ml/20fl oz/2½ cups juice. Heat the mixture gently, stirring, until the sugar dissolves.

Bring to the boil and boil hard for 10 minutes or until setting point is reached. Remove from the heat and pour into warmed sterilized jars, cover and seal.

RUMTOPF

This traditional German preserve is made by storing fresh berries in a mix of white rum and sugar for 2 months in a cool dark place.

SMOOTHIES AND DRINKS

Many delectable blended drinks can be made easily with the help of a food processor, blender or juice extractor.

RASPBERRY AND OATMEAL SMOOTHIE

This sensuously smooth drink is full of wholesome goodness.

Spoon 22.5ml/1½ tbsp oatmeal into a heatproof bowl. Pour in 120ml/4fl oz/½ cup boiling water and leave to stand for 10 minutes. Put the soaked oats in a blender and add 150g/5 oz/1½ cups raspberries, 5ml/1 tsp honey and about 30ml/2 tbsp of yogurt. Whizz until smooth and creamy. Pour the smoothie into a large glass, swirl in 10ml/2 tsp yogurt and top with a few extra whole raspberries.

BLUEBERRY MERINGUE CRUMBLE

This drink combines fresh tangy fruit, crisp sugary meringue and ice cream in one milkshake. Put 150g/5oz/1½ cups fresh blueberries and 15ml/1 tbsp icing (confectioners') sugar in a food processor with 60ml/ 4 tbsp water and blend until smooth. Transfer the purée to a small bowl. Put 250ml/8fl oz/ 1 cup natural (plain) yogurt, 200ml/7fl oz/1 cup full cream (whole) milk and 30ml/2 tbsp lime juice in the food processor and process until combined. Add 35g/1¼ oz crushed meringues and blend until smooth. Pour alternate layers of the milkshake, blueberry syrup and crushed meringues into tall glasses and top with a few blueberries.

SIMPLY STRAWBERRY

Nothing evokes a sense of summer than the flavour of sweet, juicy strawberries.

Hull 400g/14oz/3½ cups strawberries and place them in a food processor with 30ml/ 2 tbsp of icing (confectioners') sugar. Blend to a smooth purée. Add 200g/7 oz/1 cup Greek (US-strained plain) yogurt and 60ml/4 tbsp single (light)

cream and blend again until smooth and frothy. Check the sweetness, adding a little more sugar if you find the flavour too sharp. Pour into glasses and serve decorated with extra sliced strawberries.

BERRIED TREASURE

Cranberries and raspberries are fast becoming a juice classic. This recipe uses raspberry conserve to add sweetness, in place of sugar or honey.

Push 250g/9 oz/1¼ cups raspberries through a juicer, then do the same with 45ml/ 3 tbsp raspberry conserve and 250g/9oz/1¼ cups cranberries. Pour the juice into tall glasses

and top up with soda water or sparkling mineral water and serve immediately.

ICE COOL CURRANT

Intensely flavoured blackcurrants, whizzed in a blender with crushed ice, make a drink so thick and slushy that you might want to serve it with long spoons.

Put 125g/4½ oz/²/₃ cup blackcurrants and 60ml/4 tbsp light muscovado (brown) sugar in a pan. (There is no need to string the blackcurrants first.) Add a good pinch of mixed (apple pie) spice and pour in 100ml/3½ fl oz/½ cup water. Bring the mixture to the boil

and cook for 2–3 minutes until the blackcurrants are completely soft. Press the mixture through a sieve into a bowl, squeezing the pulp in with the back of a dessertspoon to extract as much juice as possible. Set aside to cool completely.

Put 225g/8 oz crushed ice in a food processor with the cooled juice and process for about 1 minute until slushy. Pour into glasses and serve immediately.

If you have a glut of blackcurrants, make twice the quantity of the juice and keep in the refrigerator for up to 1 week.

SOUPS AND SAVOURIES

THE SWEET, YET TART TASTE OF BERRIES

COMBINES SURPRISINGLY WELL WITH SAVOURY

FOODS. THEY ARE A WONDERFUL CONTRAST TO

RICH MEAT AND POULTRY, AND MAKE REFRESHING

AND COLOURFUL CHILLED SOUPS

BEETROOT AND CRANBERRY SOUP WITH BRIOCHE

Although it sounds complex, this soup is ridiculously easy to make. The sweet, earthy flavour of
fresh, cooked beetroot is combined with zesty orange and tart cranberry.

Serves 4

350g/12oz cooked beetroot,
(beet) roughly chopped
grated rind and juice of 1 orange
600ml/20fl oz/2½ cups
unsweetened cranberry juice
450ml/¾ pint/scant 2 cups
Greek (US-strained plain)
yogurt
a little tabasco
4 slices brioche
60ml/4 tbsp mascarpone
salt and ground black pepper
fresh mint sprigs and fresh
cranberries, to garnish

COOK'S TIP
If the oranges you use are a
little tart, add a pinch of
sugar to the soup.

Energy 365kcal/1544kJ; Protein 13.9g;
Carbohydrate 63.7g, of which sugars 40.5g;
Fat 8g, of which saturates 1.9g; Cholesterol
18mg; Calcium 316mg; Fibre 1.7g; Sodium
331mg

Purée the beetroot with the orange rind and juice, half the cranberry
juice and the yogurt in a food processor or blender until smooth.

Press the purée through a sieve (strainer) into a clean bowl. Stir in
the remaining cranberry juice, tabasco and salt and pepper to taste.
Chill for at least 2 hours.

Preheat the grill (broiler). Using a large pastry cutter, stamp a round
out of each slice of brioche and toast until golden. Ladle the soup into
bowls and top each with brioche and mascarpone. Garnish with mint
and fresh cranberries.

RED BERRY SOUP WITH CREAM

Utterly simple to prepare, it can be made using a blend of various red berries. Served cold with a swirl of cream in each bowl, the soup is sweet and tangy.

Serves 6

*400g/14oz/3½ cups
redcurrants
450g/1lb/3 cups raspberries,
plus a few extra, to decorate
100–150g/3¾–5oz/½–¾ cup
sugar (depending on the
sweetness of the fruit)
550ml/18fl oz/2½ cups
blackcurrant juice
45ml/3 tbsp cornflour
(cornstarch)
250ml/8fl oz/1 cup double
(heavy) cream
10ml/2 tsp vanilla sugar*

Put the currants, berries, sugar and 500ml/17fl oz/generous 2 cups of the blackcurrant juice into a pan and add 750ml/1¼ pints/3 cups water. Bring the mixture to the boil and cook over a medium-high heat for 3 minutes. Pour the fruit and juice through a strainer set over a pan. Use a wooden spoon to press through as much berry juice as possible.

In a small bowl, mix the cornflour with the remaining blackcurrant juice. Stir the cornflour mixture into the berry juice. Place the pan over a medium heat and bring the juice to the boil, stirring, until it thickens.

Pour the cream into a bowl and stir in the vanilla sugar. Pour the soup into individual bowls and spoon 30ml/2 tbsp cream into each bowl, swirling it slightly. Sprinkle each bowl with a few fresh raspberries and serve.

Energy 383kcal/1606kJ; Protein 3.1g;
Carbohydrate 44g, of which sugars 37.1g;
Fat 23g, of which saturates 14.1g;
Cholesterol 57mg; Calcium 84mg; Fibre
3.6g; Sodium 25mg.

FRUIT-FILLED SOUFFLÉ OMELETTE

This impressive dish is surprisingly quick and easy to make. The creamy omelette fluffs up in the pan, flops over to envelop its filling of fruits in liqueur and then slides gracefully on to the plate.

Serves 2

75g/3oz/¾ cup strawberries, hulled
45ml/3 tbsp Kirsch, brandy or Cointreau
3 eggs, separated
30ml/2 tbsp caster (superfine) sugar
45ml/3 tbsp double (heavy) cream, whipped
a few drops of vanilla extract
25g/1oz/2 tbsp butter
icing (confectioners') sugar, sifted

Energy 289kcal/1201kJ; Protein 6.8g;
Carbohydrate 12.3g, of which sugars 12.3g;
Fat 20.5g, of which saturates 10.9g;
Cholesterol 229mg; Calcium 47mg; Fibre
0.3g; Sodium 126mg.

Cut the strawberries in half and place in a bowl. Pour over 30ml/2 tbsp of the liqueur and set aside to marinate.

Beat the egg yolks and sugar together until pale and fluffy, then fold in the whipped cream and vanilla extract. Whisk the egg whites in a very large, grease-free bowl until stiff, then carefully fold in the yolks.

Melt the butter in an omelette pan. When sizzling, pour in the egg mixture and cook until set underneath, shaking occasionally. Spoon on the strawberries and liqueur and, tilting the pan, slide the omelette so that it folds over.

Carefully slide the omelette on to a warm serving plate, spoon over the remaining liqueur and sprinkle icing sugar over it. Cut the omelette in half, transfer to two warmed plates and eat immediately.

MACKEREL WITH GOOSEBERRY RELISH

Mackerel and gooseberries work well together, with the tart gooseberries cutting through the rich oiliness of the mackerel. It makes an unusual but satisfying lunch.

Serves 4
4 whole mackerel
60ml/4 tbsp olive oil

For the relish
250g/9oz gooseberries
25g/1oz/2 tbsp soft light brown sugar
5ml/1 tsp wholegrain mustard
salt and ground black pepper

> **COOK'S TIP**
> Turn the grill (broiler) on well in advance as the fish need a fierce heat to cook quickly. If you like the fish but hate the smell, try barbecuing outside.

Energy 576kcal/2390kJ; Protein 38.1g; Carbohydrate 8.4g, of which sugars 8.4g; Fat 43.5g, of which saturates 8.2g; Cholesterol 108mg; Calcium 43mg; Fibre 1.5g; Sodium 128mg.

For the relish, wash and trim the gooseberries and then roughly chop them. Cook the gooseberries in a little water with the sugar. A thick and chunky purée will form. Add the mustard and season to taste.

Preheat the grill (broiler) to high. Using a sharp knife, slash the fish two or three times down each side then season and brush with the olive oil. Grill (broil) the fish for about 4 minutes on each side until cooked. To check that they are cooked properly, use a small sharp knife to pierce the skin and check for uncooked flesh.

Place the mackerel on warmed plates and spread generous dollops of the gooseberry relish over them. Pass the remaining sauce around at the table.

STRAWBERRY AND SMOKED VENISON SALAD

This tasty salad combines strawberries, balsamic vinegar and smoked venison. The tang of the vinegar sets off the sweetness of the strawberries, and adds a fruity contrast to the rich venison.

Serves 4
12 large ripe strawberries
2.5ml/½ tsp caster (superfine) sugar
5ml/1 tsp balsamic vinegar
8 thin slices of smoked venison
mixed salad leaves

For the dressing
10ml/2 tsp olive oil
5ml/1 tsp balsamic vinegar
splash of strawberry wine or cordial (optional)
salt and ground black pepper

Slice the strawberries vertically into three or four pieces then place in a bowl with the sugar and balsamic vinegar. Leave for 30 minutes.

Meanwhile, make the dressing by placing the olive oil and balsamic vinegar in a small bowl and whisking them together with the wine or cordial, if you are using it. Add salt and ground black pepper to taste.

Cut the smoked venison into little strips. Mix the salad leaves together then toss with the dressing. Distribute the salad leaves among four plates, sprinkle with the strawberries and venison and serve immediately.

Energy 116kcal/486kJ; Protein 11.6g; Carbohydrate 3.1g, of which sugars 3.1g; Fat 6.8g, of which saturates 1.2g; Cholesterol 25mg; Calcium 16mg; Fibre 0.6g; Sodium 31mg.

ROE DEER MEDALLIONS WITH REDCURRANTS

With roe deer the fillet is much smaller, so ask for the medallions to be cut from the thick end of the fillet and allow two per person. The redcurrant sauce is a tasty and colourful addition to the dish.

Serves 4

about 800g/1¾lb venison fillet, preferably roe deer, cut into 8 medallions
15g/½oz/1 tbsp butter
15ml/1 tbsp vegetable oil
salt and ground black pepper

For the sauce

200ml/7fl oz/scant 1 cup venison or beef stock
150ml/¼ pint/⅔ cup port
100ml/3½fl oz/scant ½ cup double (heavy) cream
30ml/2 tbsp redcurrants
a knob of butter

Preheat the oven to 200°C/400°F/Gas 6. Season the venison medallions with salt and pepper. Heat the butter and oil in a large frying pan, add the medallions and quickly sear on both sides, then put on a baking tray and set aside.

Add the stock to the pan, stirring to deglaze and scraping up any sediment from the bottom of the pan. Add the port and cream, stir well together, then cook until reduced by half. Season the sauce with salt and pepper to taste. Add the redcurrants and a knob of butter.

Roast the medallions in the oven for 4–5 minutes, according to size, until slightly underdone. Place the medallions on individual warmed serving plates or a serving dish, pour a little sauce over each and serve the remaining sauce separately.

Energy 337kcal/1407kJ; Protein 30.1g; Carbohydrate 3.8g, of which sugars 3.8g; Fat 20.3g, of which saturates 10.9g; Cholesterol 106mg; Calcium 23mg; Fibre 0.2g; Sodium 95mg.

ROAST CHICKEN WITH LINGONBERRIES

This variation of the traditional Sunday roast features sliced, roast chicken served cold with potato salad, and a sauce of tart-sweet lingonberries, a meal that's easy on the cook.

Serves 6–8

1 roasting chicken, about
   1.6–2kg/3½–4½lb
½ lemon
60ml/4 tbsp chopped parsley
65g/2½oz/5 tbsp butter,
   softened
250ml/8fl oz/1 cup chicken
   stock or water
350g/12oz/1½ cups
   unsweetened lingonberries
100–150g/3¾–5oz/½–¾ cup
   caster (superfine) sugar, to
   taste
salt and white pepper

COOK'S TIP
Look for frozen packs of unsweetened lingonberries in Scandinavian speciality shops, and sweeten to taste. A ready-made lingonberry preserve could also be used.

Preheat the oven to 220°C/425°F/Gas 7. Rinse the chicken and pat dry inside and out with kitchen paper. Rub with lemon and season with salt and pepper.

Mix together the parsley and 40g/1½oz/3 tbsp of the butter and spread this inside the chicken. Close the opening with a skewer or fine string. Pour half the chicken stock or water into a roasting pan and place the chicken, breast side up, on a rack in the pan. Melt the remaining butter and brush half of it over the chicken. Roast for 30 minutes.

Lower the oven temperature to 180°C/350°F/Gas 4. Pour the remaining stock or water into the pan. Baste the chicken with the remaining melted butter and the pan juices and continue to cook for a further 30–40 minutes, until the juices run clear when the thickest part of the thigh is pierced. Remove from the oven, cover and leave to cool. Refrigerate the cooled chicken until ready to slice for serving.

Place the lingonberries in a bowl. Add the sugar a little at a time, stirring until the sugar thoroughly dissolves and the fruit is mashed. Add more sugar to taste and chill the lingonberries until ready to serve.

Remove the chicken from the refrigerator half an hour before serving so that the meat is not too chilled. Just before you are ready to eat, carve the chicken and arrange the slices, together with the whole legs and wings on a serving platter. Serve with a potato salad and the lingonberry sauce.

Energy 405kcal/1682kJ; Protein 24.9g; Carbohydrate 15.3g, of which sugars 15.3g; Fat 27.4g, of which saturates 10.2g; Cholesterol 145mg; Calcium 36mg; Fibre 1.4g; Sodium 151mg.

TURKEY AND CRANBERRY BUNDLES

After the traditional Christmas or Thanksgiving meal, it is easy to end up with lots of turkey leftovers and half-empty jars of cranberry sauce. These filo pastry parcels are a great way of using them up.

Serves 6
450g/1lb cooked turkey, cut
 into chunks
115g/4oz/1 cup diced brie
30ml/2 tbsp cranberry sauce
30ml/2 tbsp chopped fresh
 parsley
9 sheets filo pastry, 45 × 28cm/
 18 × 11in each, thawed if
 frozen
50g/2oz/¼ cup butter, melted
salt and ground black pepper
green salad, to serve

Preheat the oven to 200°C/400°F/Gas 6. Mix the turkey, diced brie, cranberry sauce and chopped parsley. Season with salt and pepper.

Cut the filo sheets in half widthways and trim to make 18 squares. Layer three pieces of pastry together, brushing them with a little melted butter so that they stick together. Repeat with the remaining filo squares to give six pieces.

Divide the turkey mixture among the pastry, making neat piles on each piece. Gather up the pastry to enclose the filling in small bundles. Place on a baking sheet, brush with a little melted butter and bake for 20 minutes, or until the pastry is crisp and golden. Serve hot or warm with a green salad.

Energy 304kcal/1274kJ; Protein 27.3g; Carbohydrate 16.6g, of which sugars 3.9g; Fat 14.3g, of which saturates 8.5g; Cholesterol 95mg; Calcium 91mg; Fibre 0.8g; Sodium 204mg.

HOT DESSERTS

BERRIES, EITHER ALONE OR WITH OTHER FRUITS,
MAKE BRILLIANT FILLINGS FOR COMFORTING
WINTER CRUMBLES, AND SWEET CRÊPES. THEIR
SOFT, JUICY TEXTURE MAKES A MOUTHWATERING
COMBINATION WITH CREAMY CUSTARD TO
CREATE DELICIOUS SOUFFLÉS AND CREME BRÛLÉE

RASPBERRY BRÛLÉE

Cracking through the caramelized top of a crème brûlée to reveal the creamy custard underneath is so satisfying. These ones have the added bonus of a rich, fruity custard packed with raspberries.

Serves 4

115g/4oz/1 cup fresh
   raspberries
300ml/10fl oz/1¼ cups ready-
   made fresh custard (or for
   fresh custard see p61)
75g/3oz caster (superfine) sugar

COOK'S TIP
You can now buy little gas blow torches for use in the kitchen. They make quick work of caramelizing the sugar on top of the brûlées – and are also fun to use!

Energy 322kcal/1352kJ; Protein 9.8g;
Carbohydrate 45.8g, of which sugars 45.8g;
Fat 12.1g, of which saturates 6.3g;
Cholesterol 179mg; Calcium 287mg; Fibre
1.6g; Sodium 97mg.

Tip the raspberries into a large bowl and crush with a fork. Add the custard and gently fold in until combined.

Divide the mixture between four 120ml/4fl oz/½ cup ramekin dishes. Cover each one with clear film (plastic wrap) and chill in the refrigerator for 2–3 hours.

Preheat the grill (broiler) to high. Remove the clear film from the ramekin dishes and place them on a baking sheet. Sprinkle the sugar over the custards and grill (broil) for about 3–4 minutes, or until the sugar has caramelized.

Remove the custards from the grill and set aside for a few minutes to allow the sugar to harden, then serve.

BLUEBERRY SOUFFLÉ

Blueberry jam is the star attraction in this light and airy dessert. You could also substitute with cloudberry jam, which is available in specialist Scandinavian stores.

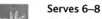

Serves 6–8
50g/2oz/4 tbsp unsalted
(sweet) butter, plus extra for
greasing
60ml/4 tbsp plain (all-purpose)
flour
475ml/16fl oz/2 cups milk
4 egg yolks and 6 egg whites
275g/10oz/1 cup blueberry or
cloudberry jam

Preheat the oven to 180°C/350°F/Gas 4. Grease an 18cm/7in soufflé dish with butter, or six individual dishes. Melt the butter in a pan, add the flour and cook over a low heat for 30 seconds, stirring to make a roux. Slowly add the milk, stirring continuously, to form a smooth sauce. Cook until the sauce boils and thickens.

Remove the sauce from the heat, leave to cool slightly then stir in the egg yolks. Add the blueberry or cloudberry jam and turn into a large bowl.

In a large, separate bowl, whisk the egg whites until stiff then, using a metal spoon, fold them into the sauce. Put the mixture into the prepared soufflé dish and bake in the oven for about 20 minutes until risen. Serve the soufflé immediately.

Energy 284kcal/1198kJ; Protein 6.7g; Carbohydrate 44.9g, of which sugars 37.4g; Fat 9g, of which saturates 4.7g; Cholesterol 118mg; Calcium 102mg; Fibre 0.2g; Sodium 129mg.

SWEET CRÊPES

These wonderfully addictive crêpes consist of a large, thin pancake, filled with strawberries, then rolled up and topped with icing sugar, whipped cream and chocolate.

Serves 3–4

200g/7oz/generous 1⅔ cups plain (all-purpose) flour
2 eggs
pinch of salt
500ml/17fl oz/2¼ cups milk
butter or oil, for frying

For the topping and filling

1 can of strawberries in syrup (400g/14oz can)
100g/3¾oz icing (confectioners') sugar
whipped cream, to serve
chocolate topping/syrup (in bottle)

Combine the flour and eggs in a bowl. Add the salt and gradually add the milk while whisking the batter. The mixture should be the consistency of double (heavy) cream; if it is too thin, add more flour, and if it is too thick, add more milk.

Heat a small amount of butter or oil in a non-stick frying pan over medium heat. Pour a ladleful of batter into the pan and spread it evenly by moving the pan from side to side. Cook for about 2–3 minutes until golden underneath, then flip the pancake over and cook on the other side. Remove and keep warm while you make the other pancakes.

Place 5–6 strawberries in the middle of each pancake and roll them up. To serve, dust with icing sugar and top with a dollop of whipped cream and the chocolate topping.

Energy 644kcal/2707kj; Protein 14;
Carbohydrate 89g, of which sugars 51g; Fat
28g, of which saturates 5g; Cholesterol
84mg; Calcium 239mg; Fibre 2.0g; Sodium
201mg.

SUMMER BERRIES IN SABAYON GLAZE

*This luxurious combination of summer berries under a light and fluffy liqueur sauce is lightly grilled
to form a crisp, caramelized topping. It makes an impressive after-dinner dessert.*

Serves 4

*450g/1lb/4 cups mixed summer
 berries, or soft fruit
4 egg yolks
50g/2oz/¼ cup vanilla sugar or
 caster (superfine) sugar
120ml/4fl oz/½ cup liqueur,
 such as Cointreau or Kirsch, or
 a white dessert wine*

COOK'S TIP
Fresh or frozen berries can
be used in this dessert. If
you use frozen berries,
defrost them in a sieve
(strainer) over a bowl to
allow the juices to drip. Stir
a little juice into the fruit
before dividing among the
flameproof dishes.

Arrange the mixed summer berries or soft fruit in four individual
flameproof dishes. Preheat the grill (broiler).

Whisk the yolks in a large bowl with the sugar and liqueur or wine.
Place over a pan of hot water and whisk constantly until the mixture
is thick, fluffy and pale.

Pour equal quantities of the yolk mixture into each dish. Place under
the grill (broiler) for 1–2 minutes, until just turning brown. Add an extra
splash of liqueur, if you like, and serve immediately.

Energy 235kcal/984kJ; Protein 3.9g;
Carbohydrate 27.1g, of which sugars 27.1g;
Fat 5.6g, of which saturates 1.6g;
Cholesterol 202mg; Calcium 48mg; Fibre
1.2g; Sodium 18mg.

APPLE AND BLACKBERRY CRUMBLE

Autumn heralds the harvest of apples and succulent wild berries. The pinhead oatmeal in the topping makes this classic dessert especially crunchy and flavoursome.

Serves 6–8
900g/2lb cooking apples
450g/1lb/4 cups blackberries
squeeze of lemon juice
    (optional)
175g/6oz/scant 1 cup
    granulated (white) sugar

For the topping
115g/4oz/½ cup butter
115g/4oz/1 cup wholemeal
    (whole-wheat) flour
50g/2oz/½ cup fine or
    medium pinhead oatmeal
50g/2oz/¼ cup soft light
    brown sugar
a little grated lemon rind
    (optional)

Preheat the oven to 200°C/400°F/Gas 6. To make the crumble topping, rub the butter into the flour, and then add the oatmeal and brown sugar and continue to rub in until the mixture begins to stick together, forming large crumbs. Mix in the grated lemon rind, if using.

Peel, core and slice the cooking apples into wedges. Put the apples, blackberries, lemon juice (if using), 30ml/2 tbsp water and the sugar into a shallow ovenproof dish, about 2 litres/3½ pints/9 cups capacity.

Cover the fruit with the topping. Sprinkle with a little cold water. Bake in the oven for 15 minutes, then reduce the heat to 190°C/375°F/Gas 5 and cook for another 15–20 minutes until crunchy and brown on top. Serve hot.

Energy 470Kcal/1974kJ; Protein 5.1g; Carbohydrate 78.2g, of which sugars 60.3g; Fat 17.2g,
of which saturates 10g; Cholesterol 41mg; Calcium 71mg; Fibre 7g; Sodium 128mg

COLD DESSERTS

BRILLIANTLY RED AND BLACK BERRIES BRING

A VIBRANT SPLASH OF COLOUR TO CREAMY

PAVLOVA OR THE CLASSIC SUMMER PUDDING.

USE THEM TO DELICATELY SCENT MOUSSES,

AND ADD A REFRESHING FRUITY FLAVOUR

TO ICES AND GRANITA

RASPBERRY GRANITA

This vibrant bright red granita looks spectacular. Served solo, it excellent for anyone on a fat-free diet. For something more indulgent, serve with whole berries and creme fraiche or clotted cream.

Serves 6
115g/4oz/½ cup caster (superfine) sugar
300ml/½ pint/1¼ cups water
500g/1¼lb/4¼ cups raspberries, hulled, plus extra, to decorate
juice of 1 lemon
little sifted icing (confectioners') sugar, for dusting

COOK'S TIP
For a granita with a little extra oomph, stir in 45ml/ 3 tbsp cassis, but don't be tempted to add more or the granita will not freeze.

Energy 96kcal/413kJ; Protein 1.3g; Carbohydrate 23.9g, of which sugars 23.9g; Fat 0.3g, of which saturates 0.1g; Cholesterol 0mg; Calcium 31mg; Fibre 2.1g; Sodium 4mg.

Bring the sugar and water to a boil, stirring occasionally until the sugar has dissolved. Pour the sugar syrup into a bowl, leave to cool, then chill.

Purée the raspberries and spoon the purée into a fine sieve (strainer) set over a large bowl. Press the purée through the sieve and discard the seeds. Scrape the purée into a measuring jug, stir in the sugar syrup and lemon juice and top up to 1 litre/1¾ pints/4 cups with cold water.

Pour the mixture into a large plastic container so that the depth is no more than 2.5cm/1in. Cover and freeze for 2 hours until the mixture around the sides of the container is mushy.

Using a fork, break up the ice crystals and mash finely. Return to the freezer for 2 hours, beating every 30 minutes until the ice forms fine, even crystals. Spoon into tall glass dishes and decorate with extra raspberries dusted with a little sifted icing sugar, if you wish.

STRAWBERRY SNOW

Strawberries have a delicate, fragrant taste and most desserts featuring them are best eaten soon after they are made so that the fruit doesn't lose its texture.

Serves 4

120ml/4fl oz/½ cup water
15ml/1 tbsp powdered gelatine
300g/11oz/2¾ cups
   strawberries, crushed lightly
250ml/8fl oz/1 cup double
   (heavy) cream
4 egg whites
90g/3½oz/½ cup caster
   (superfine) sugar
halved strawberries, to decorate

COOK'S TIP
Strawberry Snow freezes well and can then be served as an iced parfait. To make this, spoon the mixture into a loaf tin (pan) lined with clear film (plastic wrap) and freeze for a couple of hours, until it is firm.

Energy 443kcal/1841kJ; Protein 7.8g; Carbohydrate 29.1g, of which sugars 29.1g; Fat 33.7g, of which saturates 20.9g; Cholesterol 86mg; Calcium 56mg; Fibre 0.8g; Sodium 81mg.

Put the water in a small bowl and sprinkle in the gelatine. Stand the bowl over a pan of hot water and heat gently until dissolved. Remove the bowl from the pan and leave to cool slightly.

Put half the crushed strawberries in a pan and bring to the boil. Remove from the heat, then stir in the dissolved gelatine. Chill in the refrigerator for about 2 hours until syrupy.

Pour the cream into a bowl and whisk until it holds its shape. Whisk the egg whites until stiff, gradually adding the sugar as they rise. Fold the egg whites into the cooled strawberry mixture, then fold in the remaining crushed strawberries followed by the whipped cream.

Turn into individual serving dishes and serve immediately or chill until required. Serve decorated with halved strawberries.

BLACKBERRY ICE CREAM

There could scarcely be fewer ingredients in this delicious, vibrant ice cream. Frozen blackberries can be used for the purée but you will need to increase the cooking time to 10 minutes and stir often.

Serves 4–6
500g/1¼lb/4¼ cups
blackberries, hulled, plus
extra, to decorate
75g/3oz/6 tbsp caster
(superfine) sugar
30ml/2 tbsp water
300ml/½ pint/1¼ cups
whipping cream

Put the blackberries, sugar and water in a pan. Cover and simmer for 5 minutes until just soft. Tip the fruit into a sieve (strainer) placed over a bowl and press it through the mesh. Leave to cool, then chill.

By hand: Whip the cream until it is just thick but still soft enough to fall from a spoon, then mix it with the chilled fruit purée. Pour the mixture into a plastic freezerproof container and freeze for 2 hours.

Using an ice cream maker: Churn the chilled purée for 10–15 minutes until it is thick, then gradually pour in the cream.

By hand: Mash the mixture with a fork, to break up the ice crystals. Return it to the freezer for 4 hours more, beating the mixture again after 2 hours.

Using an ice cream maker: Continue to churn the ice cream until it is firm enough to scoop. Served, decorated with extra blackberries.

COOK'S TIP
If you make the ice cream in a machine, don't be tempted to add the cream with the fruit or the mixture will be come buttery by the time it has been churned and is stiff enough to scoop.

Energy 261kcal/1081kJ; Protein 1.8g; Carbohydrate 18.7g, of which sugars 18.7g; Fat 20.3g, of which saturates 12.6g; Cholesterol 52mg; Calcium 70mg; Fibre 2.6g; Sodium 15mg.

CRANBERRY AND WHITE CHOCOLATE ICE CREAM

A traditional American combination – the creamy sweet white chocolate ice cream complements the slight sharpness of the ruby-red fruits for a richly contrasting marbled ice cream.

Serves 6

*150g/5oz/1¼ cups frozen
    cranberries*
*125g/4½oz/scant ¾ cup caster
    (superfine) sugar*
4 egg yolks
5ml/1 tsp cornflour (cornstarch)
*300ml/½ pint/1¼ cups semi-
    skimmed (low-fat) milk*
150g/5oz white chocolate
5ml/1 tsp vanilla extract
*200ml/7fl oz/scant 1 cup
    double (heavy) cream*
extra cranberries, to decorate

> **COOK'S TIP**
> If you do not have an ice cream maker, mix the cooled chocolate custard and cream by hand and freeze until the mixture thickens. Mix in the cooled cranberries and diced chocolate and stir to combine. Freeze again until firm enough to scoop.

Put the cranberries into a pan with 60ml/4 tbsp water and cook uncovered for 5 minutes until softened. Drain off any fruit juices, mix in 60ml/4 tbsp of the sugar and leave to cool.

Whisk the egg yolks, remaining sugar and cornflour together in a bowl until thick and pale. Pour the milk into a heavy pan, bring it just to the boil, then gradually pour it on to the egg yolk mixture, whisking constantly.

Return the mixture to the pan and cook over a gentle heat, stirring constantly until the custard thickens and is smooth. Pour it back into the bowl.

Finely chop 50g/2oz of the chocolate and set aside. Break the remainder into pieces and stir into the hot custard until melted. Mix in the vanilla extract then cover, cool and chill.

Pour the cooled chocolate custard and cream into an ice cream maker and churn until thick.

Gradually mix in the cooled cranberries and chopped chocolate and churn for a few more minutes until firm enough to scoop. Transfer to a freezer container and freeze until required.

Scoop into tall glasses and decorate with a few extra cranberries.

Energy 418kcal/1735kJ; Protein 4.2g; Carbohydrate 28g, of which sugars 17.2g; Fat 32.5g, of which saturates 19.2g; Cholesterol 125mg; Calcium 62mg; Fibre 0.3g; Sodium 144mg

RASPBERRY MOUSSE GÂTEAU

A lavish quantity of raspberries gives this gâteau its vibrant colour and full flavour. Make it at the height of summer, when raspberries are plentiful and full of flavour.

Serves 8–10

2 eggs

50g/2oz/¼ cup caster (superfine) sugar

50g/2oz/½ cup plain (all-purpose) flour

30ml/2 tbsp cocoa powder

600g/1lb 5oz/3½ cups raspberries

115g/4oz/1 cup icing (confectioners') sugar

60ml/4 tbsp whisky (optional)

300ml/½ pint/1¼ cups whipping cream

2 egg whites

Energy 238kcal/996kJ; Protein 4.4g; Carbohydrate 25g, of which sugars 20.9g; Fat 14.1g, of which saturates 8.3g; Cholesterol 70mg; Calcium 58mg; Fibre 2g; Sodium 65mg.

Preheat the oven to 180°C/350°F/Gas 4. Grease and line a 23cm/9in springform cake tin (pan). Whisk the eggs and sugar in a heatproof bowl set over a pan of gently simmering water until the whisk leaves a trail when lifted. Remove the bowl from the heat and continue to whisk the mixture for 2 minutes.

Sift the flour and cocoa powder over the mixture and fold it in with a large metal spoon. Spoon the mixture into the tin and spread it gently to the edges. Bake for 12–15 minutes until just firm.

Leave to cool, then remove the cake from the tin and place it on a wire rack. Wash and dry the tin.

Line the sides of the clean tin with a strip of greaseproof paper and carefully lower the cake back into it. Freeze until the raspberry filling is ready.

Set aside 200g/7oz/generous 1 cup of the raspberries. Put the remainder in a clean bowl, stir in the icing sugar, process to a purée in a food processor or blender. Sieve the purée into a bowl, then stir in the whisky, if using.

Whip the cream to form soft peaks. Whisk the egg whites until they are stiff. Using a large metal spoon, fold the cream, then the egg whites into the raspberry purée.

Spread half the raspberry mixture over the cake. Scatter with the reserved raspberries. Spread the remaining raspberry mixture on top and level the surface. Cover and freeze the gâteau overnight.

Transfer the gâteau to the refrigerator at least 1 hour before serving. Remove it from the tin, place on a serving plate and serve in slices.

SUMMER PUDDING

This classic pudding is wonderfully easy to make, traditionally made with leftover bread and large handfuls of freshly picked garden and hedgerow berries.

Serves 4–6

8 x 1cm/½in thick slices of day-old white bread, crusts removed

800g/1¾lb/6 cups mixed berries, such as strawberries, raspberries, blackcurrants, redcurrants and blueberries

50g/2oz/¼ cup golden caster (superfine) sugar

lightly whipped double (heavy) cream or crème fraîche, to serve

Energy 230kcal/977kJ; Protein 6.2g; Carbohydrate 51.7g, of which sugars 26.5g; Fat 1.2g, of which saturates 0g; Cholesterol 0mg; Calcium 98mg; Fibre 3g; Sodium 294mg.

Trim a slice of bread to fit in the base of a 1.2 litre/2 pint/5 cup bowl, then trim another 5–6 slices to line the sides of the bowl, making sure the bread comes up above the rim.

Place all the fruit in a pan with the sugar. Do not add any water. Cook gently for 4–5 minutes until the juices begin to run.

Allow the mixture to cool then spoon the berries, and enough of their juices to moisten, into the bread-lined bowl. Reserve any remaining juice to serve with the pudding.

Fold over the excess bread from the side of the bowl, then cover the fruit with the remaining bread, trimming to fit. Place a small plate or saucer that fits inside the bowl directly on top of the pudding. Weight it down with a 900g/2lb weight, if you have one, or use a couple of full cans.

Chill the pudding in the refrigerator for at least 8 hours. To serve, run a knife between the pudding and the bowl and turn out on to a serving plate. Spoon a few berries and any reserved juices over the top.

SUMMER FRUIT PAVLOVA

Pavlova is a stunning dessert and simple to make, too. Top it with red and black soft summer berries and plenty of crème fraîche or cream.

Serves 4

4 egg whites
a pinch of salt
225g/8oz/generous 1 cup
*   caster sugar*
5ml/1 tsp cornflour (cornstarch)
300ml/½ pint/1¼ cups crème
*   fraîche, or double (heavy)*
*   cream, whipped*
15ml/1 tbsp rose water
450g/1lb/4 cups mixed soft
*   fruits, such as blackberries,*
*   blueberries, redcurrants,*
*   raspberries or loganberries*
10ml/2 tsp icing
*   (confectioners') sugar, sifted*

Energy 394kcal/1639kJ; Protein 3g;
Carbohydrate 35g, of which sugars 32g; Fat
028g, of which saturates 18g; Cholesterol
73mg; Calcium 40mg; Fibre 05g; Sodium
47mg

Preheat the oven to 140°C/275°F/Gas 1. Cut out a 25cm/10in round of greaseproof paper and place on a baking sheet.

Whisk the egg whites with a pinch of salt in a spotlessly clean bowl until white and stiff, but not crumbly. Slowly add almost all of the sugar, whisking all the time until the mixture forms stiff, glossy peaks.

Sift the cornflour over the meringue mixture, then add the rest of the sugar and whisk briefly to combine.

Spoon the meringue on to the greaseproof paper round, making a slight indentation in the centre and soft crests around the outside.

Bake for 1–1½ hours until the meringue is firm, checking frequently after 1 hour to prevent the meringue overcooking and turning brown.

Allow the meringue to cool, then carefully peel off the greaseproof paper from the base. Transfer the meringue to a serving plate.

To make the filling, mix the crème fraîche or whipped cream with the rose water and spoon into the centre of the meringue. Pile the soft fruits on top and dust with icing sugar. Serve at once.

PASTRIES
AND CAKES

RICH AUTUMN BERRIES, COMBINED WITH CREAM

OR YOGURT, MAKE DELECTABLE FILLINGS AND

TERRIFIC TOPPINGS FOR MELT-IN-THE-MOUTH

MUFFINS, TEA-TIME CAKES, AND GORGEOUS,

FRESHLY BAKED PIES AND TARTS

STRAWBERRY CREAM SHORTBREADS

These pretty desserts are always popular. Serve them as soon as they are ready because the shortbread cookies will lose their lovely crisp texture if left to stand.

Makes 6
150g/5oz/1¼ cups strawberries
450ml/¾ pint/scant 2 cups
*   double (heavy) cream*
6 round shortbread biscuits
*   (cookies)*

VARIATION
You can use any other berry you like for this dessert – try raspberries or blueberries. Two ripe, peeled peaches will also give great results.

Energy 890Kcal/3673kJ; Protein 4g;
Carbohydrate 22g, of which sugars 10g;
Fat 88g, of which saturates 55g;
Cholesterol 225mg; Calcium 105mg;
Fibre 1.0g; Sodium 100mg.

Reserve three strawberries for decoration. Hull the remaining strawberries and cut them in half.

Put the halved strawberries in a bowl and gently crush them using the back of a fork. (Only crush the berries lightly; they should not be reduced to a purée.)

Put the cream in a large, clean bowl and whip to form soft peaks. Add the crushed strawberries and gently fold in to combine. (Do not overmix.)

Halve the reserved strawberries, then spoon the strawberry and cream mixture on top of the shortbread cookies. Decorate each one with half a strawberry and serve immediately.

BLUEBERRY AND VANILLA MUFFINS

Vanilla extract has a sweet aroma and intense flavour. In this recipe it is used to enhance the natural taste of the juicy blueberries. These muffins are perfect for a mid-afternoon treat.

Makes 12 muffins

350g/12oz/3 cups plain (all-purpose) flour
10ml/2 tsp baking powder
115g/4oz/½ cup caster (superfine) sugar
2 eggs, beaten
300ml/½ pint/1¼ cups milk
120g/4oz/½ cup butter, melted
5ml/1 tsp vanilla extract
170g/6oz/1½ cups blueberries

Preheat the oven to 200°C/400°F/Gas 6. Line the cups of a standard muffin tin (pan) with paper cases

Sift the flour and baking powder into a bowl. Stir in the sugar.

In another bowl, whisk together the eggs, milk, butter and vanilla.

Fold the egg mixture into the dry ingredients with a metal spoon, then gently stir in the blueberries.

Spoon the batter into the prepared paper cases, filling them until just below the top. Fill any empty cups half full with water to prevent burning. Bake for 20–25 minutes, until the muffins are well risen and lightly browned.

Leave the muffins in the tin for 5 minutes and then turn them out on to a wire rack to cool. Serve warm or cold with a spoonful of berry preserve. They will keep in an airtight container for up to 3 days.

Energy 243kcal/1021kJ; Protein 4.9g; Carbohydrate 35.9g, of which sugars 13.1g; Fat 9.9g, of which saturates 6g; Cholesterol 56mg; Calcium 82mg; Fibre 1.2g; Sodium 102mg.

FRESH RASPBERRY AND FIG CAKES

Beautiful purple figs, with their luscious red flesh, nestle with fresh raspberries in this delicious cake batter, which puffs up around them in a golden dome as it bakes.

Makes 8–9

140g/5oz/¾ cup fresh raspberries
15ml/1 tbsp caster (superfine) sugar
3 fresh figs
225g/8oz/2 cups plain (all-purpose) flour
10ml/2 tsp baking powder
140g/5oz/¾ cup golden (superfine) caster sugar
85g/3½oz/7 tbsp butter, melted then cooled
1 egg, beaten
285ml/½ pint/1¼ cups buttermilk
grated rind of ½ small orange

> **COOK'S TIP**
> Cakes made with fresh summer fruit are best eaten while still warm.

Energy 260kcal/1098kJ; Protein 4.7g; Carbohydrate 43.2g, of which sugars 24.2g; Fat 8.9g, of which saturates 5.4g; Cholesterol 44mg; Calcium 107mg; Fibre 1.7g; Sodium 102mg.

Preheat the oven to 180°C/350°F/Gas 4. Grease the cups of a large muffin tin (pan) or line with paper muffin cases.

Sprinkle the fresh raspberries with the caster sugar. Slice the figs vertically into eighths and set them aside with the raspberries.

Sift the flour and baking powder into a large mixing bowl and mix in the sugar. Make a well in the centre of the dry ingredients.

In another bowl, mix the cooled melted butter with the egg, buttermilk and grated orange rind. Pour this mixture into the dry ingredients and fold in gently until just blended. Do not overwork the mixture.

Set aside a few raspberries and figs. Sprinkle the remaining fruit over the surface of the batter and fold in lightly. Spoon the mixture into the tin or the paper cases, filling each not more than two-thirds full.

Lightly press the reserved fruit into the top of the batter. Bake for 22–25 minutes until the muffins are risen and golden. Leave in the tin for 5 minutes, then turn out on to a wire rack to cool.

EASY ALL-IN-ONE SPONGE

This strawberry and 'cream' cake is so quick and easy to make. Store for up to three days in an airtight container, or freeze the cakes, undecorated, for up to two months.

Serves 12

175g/6oz/1½ cups self-raising (self-rising) flour
5ml/1 tsp baking powder
175g/6oz/¾ cup soft tub margarine, plus extra for greasing
175g/6oz/scant 1 cup caster (superfine) sugar
3 eggs
15ml/1 tbsp milk
5ml/1 tsp vanilla extract

For the filling and topping

150g/5oz white chocolate chips
200g/7oz/scant 1 cup cream cheese
25g/1oz/¼ cup icing (confectioners') sugar
30ml/2 tbsp strawberry jam
12 strawberries

Energy 395kcal/1648kJ; Protein 4.7g;
Carbohydrate 39.6g, of which sugars 28.5g;
Fat 25.3g, of which saturates 15.2g;
Cholesterol 94mg; Calcium 90mg; Fibre
0.5g; Sodium 173mg.

Preheat the oven to 180°C/350°F/Gas 4. Grease and line 2 20cm/8in round shallow cake tins (pans) with baking parchment.

Sift the flour and baking powder into a large bowl, then add all the remaining cake ingredients. Beat until smooth, then divide between the tins and smooth level.

Bake for 20 minutes, or until the cakes spring back when pressed. Allow to stand for 5 minutes, then turn out on to a wire rack to go cold. Remove the lining papers.

To make the filling and topping, melt the chocolate chips in a heatproof bowl over a pan of simmering water. Remove from the heat and cool slightly, then beat in the cream cheese and icing sugar.

Spread the top of one sponge with jam. Slice 4 strawberries, then arrange them over the jam. Spread one-third of the filling over the base of the other cake. Put the cakes together. Spread the remaining topping over the cake top. Decorate with strawberries.

SMALL BLUEBERRY PIES

Delicious little blueberry pies are perfect as a dessert after a Sunday lunch. Alternatively, serve them in the afternoon with plenty of hot tea.

Makes 10

For the dough
50g/2oz/¼ cup butter
200ml/7fl oz/scant 1 cup milk
45ml/3 tbsp water
2.5ml/½ tsp salt
7.5ml/1½ tsp caster (superfine) sugar
1 small (US medium) egg
400g/14oz/3½ cups plain white (all-purpose) flour
large pinch of easy-blend (rapid-rise) dried yeast

For the filling
300–350g/11–12oz/2¾–3 cups blueberries, fresh or frozen
25g/1oz/2 tbsp caster (superfine) sugar
15ml/1 tbsp potato flour

For the glaze
150ml/¼ pint/⅔ cup smetana or crème fraîche
45ml/3 tbsp caster (superfine) sugar
icing (confectioners') sugar, for dusting

To make the dough, melt the butter in a small pan. Add the milk, water, salt and sugar and heat until warm to the finger. Pour the mixture into a large bowl. Add the egg and mix together.

Put the flour and yeast in a large bowl and mix together. Stir in the butter mixture, a little at a time, until combined. Knead the dough in the bowl for at least 5 minutes. Cover the bowl with a dish towel and leave the dough to rise in a warm place for 30 minutes until it has doubled in size.

Turn the dough on to a lightly floured surface. Cut the dough into 24 equal-sized pieces and form each piece into a ball. Leave to rest for 5–10 minutes.

Meanwhile, prepare the filling. Put the blueberries in a bowl, add the sugar and potato flour and mix together.

Preheat the oven to 200°C/400°F/Gas 6. Grease a large baking tray. Flatten each ball to a round measuring about 15cm/6in in diameter.

Place the rounds on the baking tray. Place 45ml/3 tbsp of the blueberry mixture in the centre of each round then fold a small edge up around the mixture. Bake the pies in the oven for 10–15 minutes, until golden brown.

Meanwhile, make the glaze. Put the smetana or crème fraîche and the sugar in a bowl and mix together.

When the pies are baked, gently spoon a little of the glaze over each pie. Dust the tops with sifted icing sugar. Serve hot or cold.

Energy 371kcal/1559kJ; Protein 4.4g; Carbohydrate 55.8g, of which sugars 25.7g; Fat 16g, of which saturates 4.9g; Cholesterol 8mg; Calcium 93mg; Fibre 3.2g; Sodium 228mg.

SUMMER BERRY TART

A simple crisp pastry case is all that is needed to set off this classic filling of vanilla-flavoured custard topped with luscious berry fruits.

Serves 6–8

*185g/6½oz/1⅔ cups plain
   (all-purpose) flour
pinch of salt
115g/4oz/½ cup butter, diced
1 egg yolk
30ml/2 tbsp chilled water
800g/1¾lb/4½–5 cups mixed
   summer berries
60ml/4 tbsp redcurrant jelly
30ml/2 tbsp raspberry liqueur
fresh mint leaves, to decorate
   (optional)*

For the custard

*3 egg yolks
50g/2oz/¼ cup caster
   (superfine) sugar
30ml/2 tbsp cornflour
   (cornstarch)
30ml/2 tbsp plain (all-purpose)
   flour
5ml/1 tsp vanilla extract
300ml/½ pint/1¼ cups milk
150ml/¼ pint/⅔ cup double
   (heavy) cream*

To make the pastry, sift the flour and salt into a mixing bowl. Rub or cut in the butter until the mixture resembles fine breadcrumbs. Mix the egg yolk with the chilled water and sprinkle over the dry ingredients. Mix to a firm dough.

Put the dough on to a lightly floured surface and knead for a few seconds, until smooth. Wrap in clear film (plastic wrap) and chill for 30 minutes.

Roll out the pastry and use to line a 25cm/10in petal-shaped flan tin (quiche pan) or a 23cm/9in round pan. Wrap in clear film (plastic wrap) and chill.

Put a baking sheet in the oven and preheat to 200°C/400°F/Gas 6. Prick the base of the pastry, line with foil and baking beans and bake for 15 minutes. Remove the foil and beans and bake for 10 minutes more. Leave to cool.

To make the custard, beat the egg yolks, sugar, cornflour, flour and vanilla together. Bring the milk to the boil in a pan. Slowly pour on to the egg mixture, whisking all the time. Pour the custard into the cleaned pan and cook over a low heat, stirring, until it has thickened. Return to a clean mixing bowl, cover the surface with a piece of clear film and set aside to cool. Whip the cream until thick, then fold into the custard. Spoon the custard into the pastry case and spread out evenly.

Arrange the fruit on top of the custard. Gently heat the redcurrant jelly and liqueur together until melted. Allow to cool, then brush over the fruit. Serve the tart within 3 hours of assembling, decorated with mint, if using.

Energy 432kcal/1807kJ; Protein 6.7g; Carbohydrate 47.6g, of which sugars 21.8g; Fat 25.7g, of which saturates 14.6g; Cholesterol 160mg; Calcium 130mg; Fibre 2g; Sodium 150mg.

PEACH AND BLUEBERRY PIE

With its attractive lattice pastry top, this colourful pie is bursting with plump blueberries and juicy peaches. It is good hot, or can be wrapped in its tin and transported to a picnic.

Serves 8

*225g/8oz/2 cups plain
(all-purpose) flour
2.5ml/½ tsp salt
5ml/1 tsp granulated (white)
sugar
150g/5oz/10 tbsp cold butter,
diced
1 egg yolk
30–45ml/2–3 tbsp iced water
30ml/2 tbsp milk, for glazing*

For the filling

*6 peaches, peeled, pitted
and sliced
225g/8oz/2 cups fresh
blueberries
150g/5oz/¾ cup granulated
sugar
30ml/2 tbsp fresh lemon juice
40g/1½oz/⅓ cup plain
(all-purpose) flour
pinch of grated nutmeg
25g/1oz/2 tbsp butter or
margarine, cut into pea-size
pieces*

For the pastry, sift the flour, salt and sugar into a bowl. Rub the butter into the dry ingredients until the mixture resembles breadcrumbs.

Mix the egg yolk with 30ml/2 tbsp of the iced water and sprinkle over the flour mixture. Combine with a fork until the pastry holds together. Gather the pastry into a ball and flatten into a disk. Wrap in clear film (plastic wrap) and chill for at least 20 minutes.

Roll out two-thirds of the pastry to a thickness of about 3mm/⅛in. Use to line a 23cm/9in fluted tin (pan). Trim all around, leaving a 1cm/½in overhang, then trim the edges with a sharp knife.

Roll out the remaining pastry and trimmings to a thickness of about 6mm/¼in. Cut strips 1cm/½in wide. Chill the pastry case and the strips for 20 minutes. Preheat the oven to 200°C/400°F/ Gas 6.

Line the pastry case with baking parchment and fill with dried beans. Bake until the pastry case is just set, 12–15 minutes. Remove from the oven and lift out the paper with the beans. Prick the bottom of the pastry case all over with a fork, then return to the oven and bake for 5 minutes more. Let the pastry case cool slightly before filling.

In a mixing bowl, combine the peach slices with the blueberries, sugar, lemon juice, flour and nutmeg. Spoon the fruit mixture evenly into the pastry case. Dot with the pieces of butter or margarine.

Weave a lattice top with the chilled pastry strips, pressing the ends to the baked pastry-case edge. Brush the strips with the milk.

Bake the pie for 15 minutes. Reduce the heat to 180°C/350°F/Gas 4, and continue baking until the filling is tender and bubbling and the pastry lattice is golden, about 30 minutes more.

Energy 391kcal/1640kJ; Protein 4.7g; Carbohydrate 53g, of which sugars 27.7g; Fat 19.3g, of which saturates 11.7g; Cholesterol 72mg; Calcium 86mg; Fibre 2.9g; Sodium 139mg.

INDEX